INTRODUCTION

`Lucid meanderings of the unstable mind' are works of poetry. They are words from the recesses of one's mind. Written mainly in dark times on trains, trams or any spare moment he needs to find peace in his mind, these words are words that are dysfunctional within themselves. His mind has been a mess, now after writing and discovering his soul as it were, he claims, "writing is a pathway to the soul."

ADDICT

Lifting trembling hands anticipate mouth

Soothes the pressure building fast

Create relevant issues never crouch

Explosive continuance fearing that blast

AGING

Aging comes without an invitation

Doctors love people over fifty

My hair still dark although unsure for how long

They ask about tests with gaiety

Blood tests prove quacks are on the button

Life controlled with medicinal wantonly

Heart takes the strain with life's emotion

Struggle deep rooted in recess of faculty

Blackness abounds like a shivering solution

Fleeting moments strange dreams difficulty

Aging stresses coming for but a notion

ANGER INHERENT

Reprisals imminent press aware
Youngster betrayal watching on
Social media destroying fear
Listless child beaten down

ANGEL

The Angel has come for me

Not taking me away as thought

Learn to live before death in he

Love, giving is what the Angel brought

God brings her to prove

Life is grand a life without anger

Angel becomes a shadow on the move

Dear God allow me to be near her

Teaching is a skill no school can teach

Your graciousness and patience run so deep

Luxury of life, oceans encompassing a sand laden beach

Love you bring, to give, to keep

My precious Angel has arrived

Heart open, vast and free

Giving unconditionally to show and strive

My heart closed and dark until you came to me

Pray today forever shall I be

Whilst you my Angel are still around

You hold me close, I tremble and see

The Fear coming to my head in sound

God grant me this Angel

For I will be with you forever

Your debt will be paid in full

Angel, hold me, take my fear

Love is blind, love is seeing

For the Angel that has been sent

I love anew from where comes Freedom

Take me not this day, teach me life, love, not lent

BELIEF

Belief in one's self a paradox

Finding the true you comes first

Doubting follows for time collects

Make a point in delivering fast

Deep inside the devil dwells

Make enlightened oneness cast

Promise today that this day reveals

COVER ME

Take me now fears destroy

Anger waves lolling over mind

Clutching blanket blackness coming ploy

Scrunching body contorted frame submerged

CONTRITENESS

Over life delivered o' mine

Mystery prevails to remain

People are but a sheer blink

Never cheerio nor goodbye scene

Just end no communications avail

Wonderment follows bewildering angst

Days become weeks then months

Anxiousness meaning clearing mind

Letting go flighty feelings

One minute laughing joyous

Next betrayal portrays deliberations

Instinctively fall attempting constraints

World view regains mentality

Forward looking pressure relieved

Retreating brings freedom adorning light

DARKNESS

Darkness harbours light exploitation

Missing emotive wrangling evilness

White shadows follow restriction

Essence bonding delighted sumptuousness

Mastery perfecting obsessive compunction

Sensual harangued stifled conservativeness

DEAL

Life deal me a hand

As I will surely play

Shocks of time fly my land

Blackness coming from the day

Night brings negative relief

Beer, I beg please help me feel normal

Continue until sleep arrives like a thief

Stealing the darkness another day with all

Wake to witness my tired, sad face

Bed welcomes me back to its warmth

Tossing fleeting moment's race

Mind so hard, angry rage within the mouth

Silence comes, anger deep down

Screaming in noiseless torment

Sweet angels for thee please come

Take me more than my errant

Listening to my voices

Relentless crosses with edged swords

Dictating now to make sense

Nothing ever can be real to challenges

Positive talk, lazy talk, confusion abounds angry man

Negation is content to handle

Brace over my faceless plan

Never ever happy, sad in a mangle

See straight my sweet one

This will pass into memory

Move through to feel sun

Move on the angel wings slyly

Blackness returns to lie upon

Whisky has an angel's wretchedness

Cycles moving through momentum

My worth is so worthless

DEAR SNOWDROP

Blessed snowdrop you bring life after winter

For not long your presence prevails

Your smile shines when sun cracks splinter

The air around all shared without troubles

Thanking you dear snowdrop for this day to wander

As you will be far off with no cogitations

Mother Nature takes power through surrender

DIED TODAY

A little bit of me died today

Letting go is a battle of mind

Warring sides challenge with sanctity

Let go of this area or continue blind

Faith becomes harder with implicitly

Demons say run angels say find

Missing erroneous thoughts are no pity

Soul screams loud in betrayal sound

Lost listless movements bear scarcity

Trifling limbo forever moving round

Will this day be mine or give in to mediocrity

FABLE UNTRUTH

Older wiser fable untruth

Less forward troubled past

Worried without thinking through

Emotional nervousness talking fast

Dedicated life heartfelt abuse

Victimisation comes with distaste

Hateful vengeance controlled muse

Anger fulfilling mindful haste

Wanting hidden blackness disguise

Consternation demands foolish chaste

Release devilish painful eyes

FIFTY

Half a century exited

Life still with me not yet taken

Pressure on a man as he cried

Tears of pain full memories aching

Hey old man why you still here

The voice asks waiting response

Hands on head avoiding Fear

Years come years go such a terrible loss

Happiness scoffs at the disheveled wreck

Loneliness' holds the arms to dance

Trivialness so common to no luck

Proudness, laziness, lifeless his stance

FOLLOWERS

Assuaging mediocratic disillusioned followers

Pleasurable's exiting hardened foils

Cruelest exploitative manipulating dowagers

Victorious treasured fantastical spoils

GRACIOUS SMILE

Sun catches her gracious smile

With no care for all abandon

Tenacity arises against negative rile

Beauty overcomes appearance stolen

Remarkable presence solidly exceptional

Contented spirit expressing gratification

Resourceful creative expansive soul

LIFE

That moment the feeling overwhelms

Emotive reasoning takes flight

Inside not crushed spasms

Side by side head n heart

Strolling carefree into hidden realms

Challenging creativity provides insight

LIGHT BRINGS HOPE

Light brings hope without abandon

Shining through the attic panes

Smoothly invading liken a soulful song

Heart pumps easily as ray's claim

Mighty soul for you I bequeathing

LISTLESS MIND

Listless mind demanding thought

Insight conspires ragged nonsense

Intellect reduced mentally distraught

Self deniability approving credence

MASTERING

Mastering artistically delusional momentum

Hellish demonic ritualistic driven dream

Lacking realistic normal levelled dopamine

Craving expressionist emotive outpouring

MIRRORLESS

Mirror reflection apathy control

Destructive forces mind numbing

Interest unrecognisable despairing soul

Nothingness reduced mentality ensuing

MISSING

Humanistic tribulation casting shadows

Covetousness thieving ultimately cruel

Mastery manipulator disguising commodities

Life's forbidden submerged souls

MISTAKEN HERO

Uninteresting hero worshipping fanatics

Reality falsely portraying attainment

Camera flashing life's dramatics

Miserable normality feigns entertainment

MOMENTS

That moment the feeling overwhelms

Emotive reasoning takes flight

Inside not crushed spasms

Side by side Head n heart

Strolling carefree into hidden realms

Challenging creativity provides insight

MY LOVE

Fear of losing celestial beauty only to beholding

Stolen from heavens that choose to leave planetary domain
angered those left behind

To be with a devil scorned frighteningly fallen wings
simplistically cruel in actions

Rejoice from the pyre uniting challenge of defiance for those
God's surrounding

Heaven's retribution angered with fallen gracious demise a
goddess pure and free

Thunderous bellowing could be heard between ocean to sky

Lovingly fallen gods and devils running challenging like no
mere mortal soul

Bringing wrath forcefulness in its extreme soul destructive
crassness

Love shall conquer defiantly snubbing two opposites absurdly
fighting remaining together free

NOISE

My head is full of noise
It hurts to think and see
The eyes in my head poise
Ready to take on the key

Unlocking the mysterious anxiety
Enveloping the exhausted torso
Floor swimming, writhing in agony
Take me away to live no more

Visions hurt then blackout
Wake me dearest God
Voice has lost its shout
Spoil me now spare thy rod

Will tomorrow come tortured life?
Position moving, lying o'er sink
Blood is now flowing rife

Marvelous color of hue pink

My pain is releasing now
Silence is hanging around
Noise outside, farewell pretty crows
Take me on my journey darkened

Floor now upon me rolling
Ceiling above it's getting late
Releasing my will, too unforgiven
God hold me at your gate.

PHOTOSHOP

Photoshopping megalomaniacs looking for fame

Egotistical driven lies looking for ultimate beauty

Editing to deliver falsehoods and betraying claims

Plasticity looking goddesses declaring elasticity

Punishing the art of real photography realms

Truthful deliverance non forthcoming sanctity

SANCTIMONIOUS

Sanctimonious preachers pulpit lens

Thieving unimaginable charlatan rogues

Devil defining ranking politicians

Master contrite sanction destructions

SOCIAL

Social hardships catastrophic isolation

Suicide ideation relentless consternation

Misinterpreted voices reign caution

Maligned attitudinal reserving action

SOCIAL MEDIA

Socially inadequate media failing situation

Lost sadness reckless truthful inadequacies

Like dislike cruelly disguised friendly infatuation

Choices fool disgraced trodden ideologies

STRIVE

Reality explanation fading to mist

Happiness alive yet constant fading

Flowing river never fears past

Disgruntled greed manipulates focus lasting

STRUGGLE

Struggling torso defying lesser life

Head with wounds that never heal

Body contort mission nihilistic death

Non colour explosion brain doth feel

Manipulating mind child warrior flees

Missing emotion perpetual angst beneath

Hanging intention nepenthe drawl digress

TOGETHER REUNITED

Ideals and beliefs we cannot see

Promise made, reunite guarantee

Migratory border for love to free

Adoring actions shall for us to be

Meet again millennia, lest we seek

Dissimilar faith continuum, a world so bleak

Beauty does behold the magical mystique

Different past our meeting unique

Technological bridge bade us good stead

Over oceans sailing seven seas where we bled

Pirate stories full of glory, action with rivers running red

Ships aplenty masts galore those sails carried

Shore brings carnage with despair

Lost to God on a foreign shore laying bare

Comrades taken as sea devours care

Fortune for few that left spare

Looking at beauty upon the sense
Never gazed upon complexion exquisiteness
Her skins divine a dream to caress
Adoration begins from redeeming features

Taken from rescued sands
Languishing exhausted minds
Together prevailing love sends
Ships arrive to steal him rescinds

Return to land with heartbroken dreams
All to be in loving arms
Looking to sail from prison walls
Death from destructive blades

Time comes in a special wanting
Free to be with each other not struggling
A love tale for eras they are passing
Reunited in arms for their loving

Holding sentiments forever through time

Idyllic sublimation, hearts to be divine

History delivers a tale for two hearts that join

Never lose hope for true love conveying

TRAIN RIDE

Squashed no room to breathe

Human feelings alter close to other

Anxiety rising fleeing deathly wreath

Swollen throat drowning smother

Seeking solitude swearing oath

Saving regrets failing to suffer

TRITE TALE

Miscreant behaviour

Lackadaisical errant attitude

Misty devil eyed saviour

Cretinous raving delivering rancid mood

DAVID

WALKING MINDLESS

Walking zombiefied towards the day

Sun shines bright cold chill in the air

Face grimaces eyes squint feel icy

The path shadows distinct and clear

Blasting light from cornices dry

Rising plumes from exhausts smear

Braising arms and torso against sky

Emotion awakened aligned to bear

WISTFUL

68

Angelic in her graciousness

Lustful in her bewilderment

Sensual in her listlessness

Innocence taken to procurement

WRATH

Complaints justified ungrateful mentality

Acceptance difficulties shadow mirth

Blackest soul disregards humanity

Building sentiment abolished wrath

The Beginning...

Alan Thomson